WHAT IF YOU HAD AN
Animal Tail!?

by Sandra Markle

Illustrated by
Howard McWilliam

Scholastic Inc.

For Gail Nelson
and the students
of Harwinton
Consolidated School
in Harwinton,
Connecticut

A special thank-you to Caesar the giraffe and the Giraffe House animal care team at the Maryland Zoo in Baltimore for their assistance with this book.

Photos ©: cover top and throughout: Dim Dimich/Shutterstock; cover inset: eugenesergeev/iStockphoto; cover background: Iakov Kalinin/Shutterstock; back cover: Haywiremedia/Shutterstock; 4: mhaussmann/iStockphoto; 4 inset: Pirotehnik/Thinkstock; 6: pum_eva/iStockphoto; 6 inset: Peter Chadwick/Getty Images; 8: EcoPic/iStockphoto; 8 inset: YoThin Pimpanat/Shutterstock; 10: bearacreative/iStockphoto; 10 inset: SeaPics.com; 12: EcoPic/iStockphoto; 12 inset: Fuse/Getty Images; 14: Tee-roy/iStockphoto; 14 inset: kevdog818/iStockphoto; 16: benoitb/iStockphoto; 16 inset: Crystal Venters/Dreamstime; 18: Cathy Keifer/Shutterstock; 18 inset: pawatfreeman2/Shutterstock; 20: Mitsuyoshi Tatematsu/Minden Pictures; 20 inset: Suzi Eszterhas/Minden Pictures/Getty Images; 22: Mike Parry/Minden Pictures/Getty Images; 22 inset: Otto Rogge/Getty Images; 24: Jami Tarris/Getty Images; 24 inset: JohnCarnemolla/iStockphoto

Text copyright © 2018 by Sandra Markle
Illustrations copyright © 2018 by Howard McWilliam

All rights reserved. Published by Scholastic Inc., *Publishers since 1920.* SCHOLASTIC and associated logos are trademarks and/or registered trademarks of Scholastic Inc.

The publisher does not have any control over and does not assume any responsibility for author or third-party websites or their content.

ISBN 978-1-338-20878-8

19 18 17 16   22 23

Printed in the U.S.A.   40
First edition, July 2018

Book design by Kay Petronio

What if one day when you woke up, threw back the covers, and got out of bed, something felt different? What if, overnight, you'd grown a wild animal's tail?

PEACOCK

A male peacock has a tail with feathers up to six feet long that can fan across its back. The feathers have eyelike spots in beautiful colors like blue, green, and gold. This bird sheds and regrows its tail feathers each year just in time for the mating season. The peacock uses them to win a female mate, called a peahen. The bigger the fantail and the more eyespots displayed, the better the peacock's chances of gaining a mate.

FACT

Each peacock's tail has its own special pattern of eyespots and shimmering colors.

If you had a peacock's tail, fans would always flock to see you.

SOUTH AFRICAN GROUND SQUIRREL

A South African ground squirrel's long, bushy tail is a built-in sun umbrella. The squirrel uses its tail for shade, since there are few trees or bushes in the dry places where it likes to live. This squirrel usually spends the day searching for seeds and small plants to eat. But in the summer, the temperature can get up to 114°F! So the squirrel turns its back to the sun and curls its long tail over its head. Then it has its own personal shade.

FACT

When a South African ground squirrel sees a cobra, it waves its bushy tail, and the snake leaves it alone.

If you had a South African ground squirrel's tail, you'd never need to bring an umbrella to the beach.

SCORPION

A scorpion's tail and body have an armor coat called an exoskeleton. Its tail is also tipped with a deadly stinger. When the scorpion is hunting, it uses its pincers, or it flicks its tail to pierce its prey and inject it with liquid venom. This poison stops the prey from getting away. And when the scorpion is attacked by a bigger predator, such as a snake or bird, the scorpion can use its painful sting to defend itself. Then the scorpion escapes!

FACT

Baby scorpions, called scorplings, ride on their mother's back until they develop their armor coat and produce venom.

ICE CREAM

If you had a
scorpion's tail,
you'd never have
to wait in line.

THRESHER
SHARK

A thresher shark's tail isn't just for swimming. It also makes this shark a super hunter. The top half of a thresher shark's tail is *extra* long. For some adults, this part of their tail can be as long as their body—up to about twenty feet! When it goes hunting, the thresher shark swims at a school of small fish. Then it whips its long tail over its head, striking some of the fish. *SMACK!* Just like that, the stunned fish become dinner.

A thresher shark swings its tail in just one-third of a second—about as quick as the human eye blinks.

If you had
a thresher shark's
tail, you'd be a
home-run hero!

GIRAFFE

A giraffe's tail is a record-holder. Including the tail tuft, it can be up to eight feet long! That makes it the longest tail of any land mammal. The bottom half of a giraffe's tail is a long tuft of hair. But the top half is muscle and separate tailbones. These tailbones allow the tail to bend at each joint, which is where the bones meet. So a giraffe can swish its tail to swat away any biting bugs with its long tail tuft.

FACT

Every giraffe has its own unique spot pattern all over its body—including on its long tail!

If you had a giraffe's tail, you wouldn't need a brush to paint a masterpiece.

RATTLESNAKE

A rattlesnake has a built-in alarm system at the tip of its tail. When the snake shakes its tail, it makes a noisy rattle that means "Leave me alone!" As a baby, a rattler has just a button at its tail tip. The rattle forms and grows longer as the rattlesnake gets older. Every time the snake grows and sheds its old skin, a new segment is exposed at the base of the tail, adding another part to the rattle.

FACT

When a rattlesnake rattles, it shakes its tail back and forth about sixty times a second.

If you had a rattlesnake's tail, you'd have the perfect instrument to play in a band.

BEAVER

A beaver's tail is a broad, flat paddle covered with leathery scales. An adult beaver's tail can be more than a foot long—about a third of the length of its body. In the water, a beaver's tail is the perfect rudder, steering the animal while it swims with its webbed back feet. When a predator comes close, a beaver smacks its tail hard on the water's surface to warn its family there's danger and hopefully scare away the predator.

FACT

On land, a beaver uses its strong, stiff tail as a prop while munching leaves or gnawing down trees.

If you had a beaver's tail, you'd make the biggest splash in the pool.

17

TOKAY
GECKO

A tokay gecko is usually able to hide from predators like birds or snakes. But when it's spotted and a predator grabs the reptile by the tail, the gecko uses its best escape trick—dropping off the end of its tail! The nerves in the tip of the tail make it wiggle, even though it's no longer on the gecko. While the predator checks out the piece of lost tail, the gecko makes its getaway.

FACT

A tokay gecko regrows its lost tail in less than a month and can drop it again if it needs to.

If you had a tokay gecko's tail, no one could stop you from scoring a touchdown.

SPIDER
MONKEY

A spider monkey can use its long tail to grab something and hold on. The monkey's tail helps it stay safe as it swings through the trees. Its tail muscles are so strong that the spider monkey can even dangle by just the end of its tail. It's the perfect safety line while climbing with all four feet or when there's no place to sit while the monkey is out on a limb, picking fruit to eat.

FACT

A baby spider monkey wraps its tail around its mother like a seat belt when it rides on her back.

If you had a spider monkey's tail, you'd be a star trapeze performer.

CROCODILE

A crocodile's tail is nearly half its body length and is packed with muscles. It sweeps its powerful tail side to side to propel itself forward through the water while its back feet steer. A crocodile can swim as fast as eighteen miles per hour this way! For a crocodile, speed means catching a fast fish dinner. Or charging fast enough to surprise something much bigger—like a baby hippo!

FACT

A crocodile can use its tail to launch out of the water and snatch birds or monkeys from overhanging tree branches.

If you had a crocodile tail, you could swim your way to Olympic gold.

RED
KANGAROO

A red kangaroo uses its big tail like a fifth leg while hopping. To hop, the kangaroo leans forward until its front feet are touching the ground. Next, propped up by its tail, the kangaroo swings both of its hind feet ahead of its front legs. And when it springs forward, its big tail keeps it balanced. Hopping this way, red kangaroos have been clocked traveling as fast as forty miles per hour!

FACT

When a male red kangaroo is fighting for a mate, he balances on his tail and tiptoes to look bigger.

If you had a red kangaroo's tail, you'd have no trouble standing out on the dance floor.

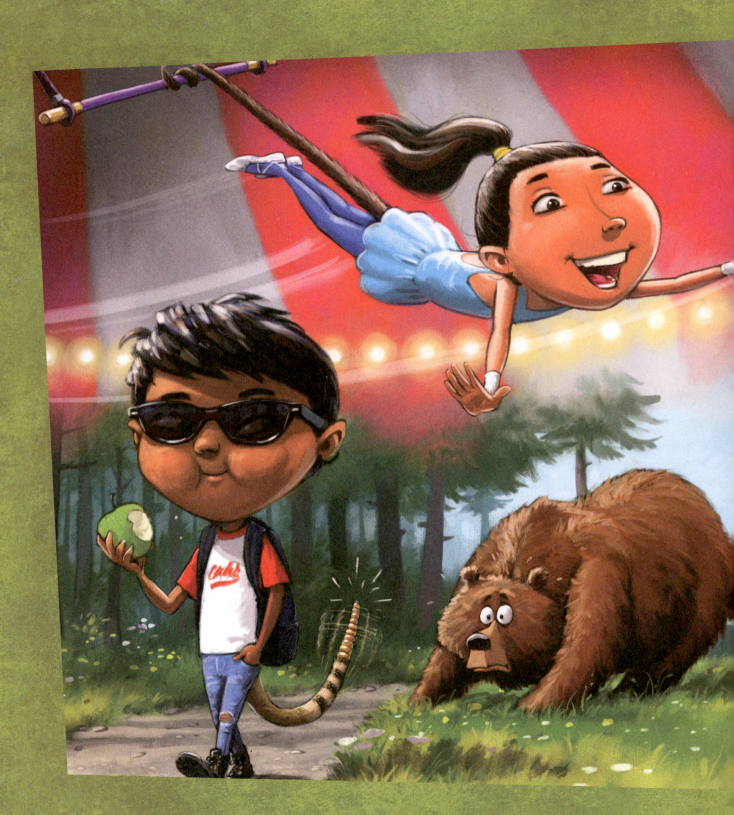

A wild animal's tail could be fun for a while. But you don't need a tail to swat flies or scare off predators. You can get by without a tail to hang from or to help you swim faster than your dinner. And you're great on your own, even

without a fantail to show off. But if you could keep a wild animal tail for more than a day, what kind would be right for you?

Luckily, you don't have to choose. You don't need a tail, because you already have a tailbone that is right for your body. Your tailbone is exactly what

you need to sit down or stand up straight. It's important for riding a bike, or even sitting cross-legged on the floor.

WHAT'S SPECIAL ABOUT YOUR TAILBONE?

Your tailbone, also called the coccyx (KAK-sicks), is the name for the last few bones of your spine. This group of bones—plus the muscles, tendons, and ligaments that attach to it—form a support system for your body. The ligaments are tough bands that hook the individual bones in your tailbone together. The tendons are flexible bands that attach the muscles to the bones.

SPINE

SACRUM

COCCYX
(TAILBONE)

This tailbone system works with the lower backbones and hip bones (pelvis) to brace your back. That supports your body's weight so you can sit up straight, even when there isn't anything to lean against.

YOUR TAILBONE NEEDS YOU!

Like any bone in your body, your tailbone can break. Falling backward and landing hard on your rear end can do it. Your tailbone can also be hurt by sports, especially those that require sitting while moving, such as rowing or bike riding. An injured tailbone makes standing and sitting *very* painful. Here are some ways to protect your tailbone:

- Don't sit sideways on just one hip.

- Sit straight and tall with your shoulders back.

- Be extra careful when walking on slippery surfaces where you might fall, like ice or wet floors.

- Don't sit for too long. Try to get up and move about every twenty minutes.

CAUTION
WET FLOOR

OTHER BOOKS IN THE SERIES

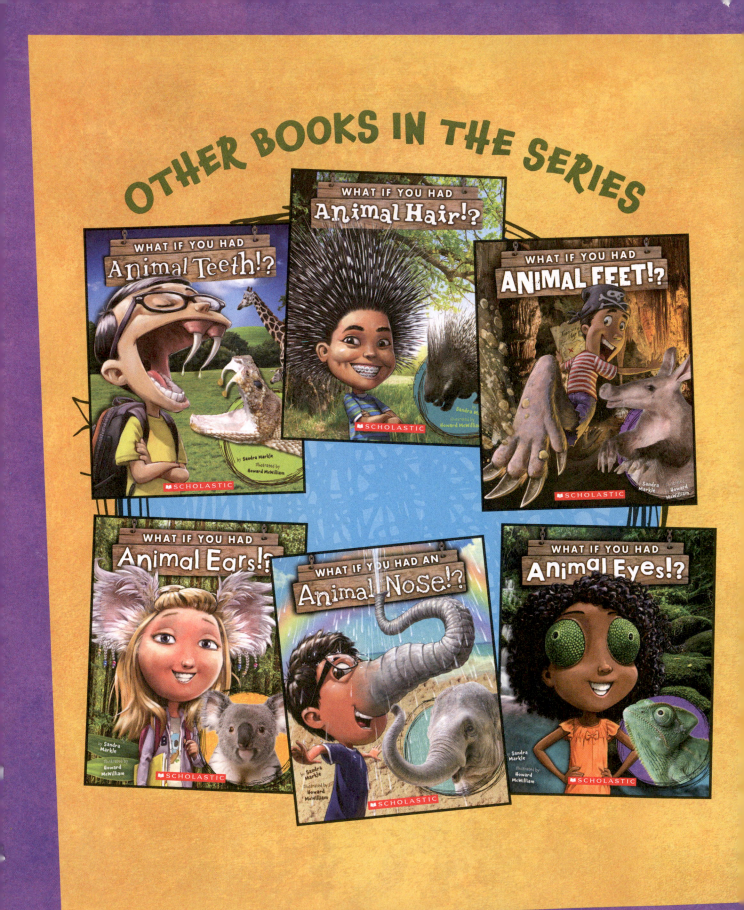

WHAT IF YOU HAD
Animal Hair!?

WHAT IF YOU HAD
Animal Teeth!?

by Sandra Markle
Illustrated by
Howard McWilliam

WHAT IF YOU HAD
ANIMAL FEET!?

Sandra Markle   Howard McWilliam

WHAT IF YOU HAD
Animal Ears!?

by Sandra Markle
Illustrated by
Howard McWilliam

WHAT IF YOU HAD AN
Animal Nose!?

by Sandra Markle
Illustrated by
Howard McWilliam

WHAT IF YOU HAD
Animal Eyes!?

Sandra Markle
Illustrated by
Howard McWilliam